One Year in Mariestad

One Year in Mariestad

William Males

Poems

Åsa Antalffy Eriksson

Illustrations

One Year in Mariestad © William Males 2013

Published and printed by: BoD

ISBN 978-91-7463-915-5

Illustrations, book design and cover: Åsa Antalffy Eriksson

lace of light

playing on the floor

beechwood forest

stone on mossy stone

the old wall in the beech woods

has lost its meaning

the emptiness

between street stones

also street

of bars

the sun makes

shadows

I draw a breath

strike what I had written

in the harbor a gull takes wing

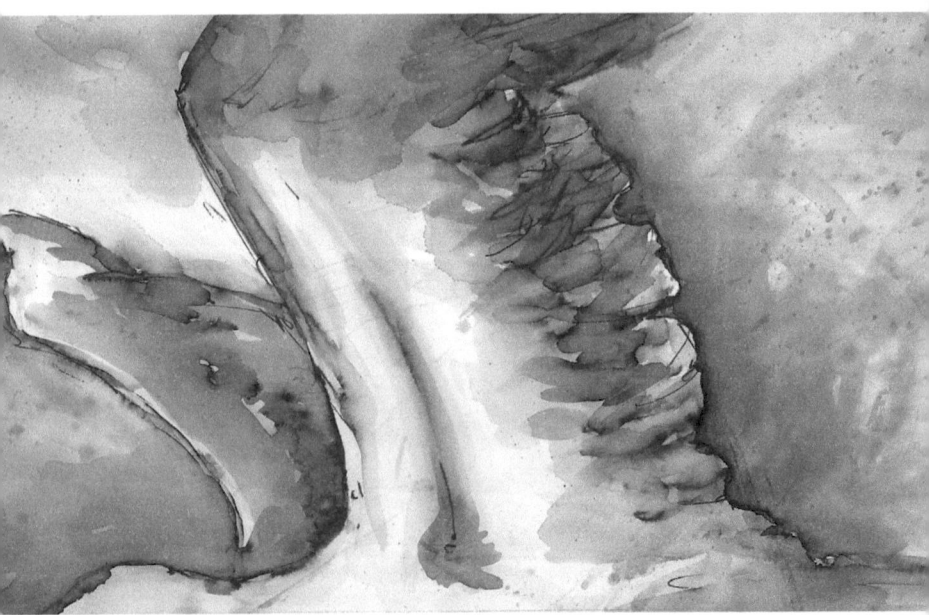

the tern and I

peering from the harbor bridge

side by side

wagtail

a restless dot

on the road

gross national product

fields of dandelions

not included

flocks of jackdaws

restless in the sky

writing nothing

distant blues

and smoldering sunset

drummed out by flagpoles

loneliness

in lighted places

a man swears into his fist

quiet darkness

I drink my tea

unsweetened

a rowboat in the dark

pulls at a point

of silver

stars constant above

TVs shimmering

in every home

flash and rumble

of the night train

in the distance city glow

this must be dawn

now the outline of a hill

a different darkness

leafy shadows

falling on the bike path

I slow down

last year's leaf

loping with the wind

tarantula

a small pond

surrounded by shadows

quiet in the storm

one leaf moving

where the breeze

touches shore

in the underpass

among scribbled symbols

I try to write

like a fisherman

I shake

my phone wire free

14 Tuesday

Imagine -
if I could plan
my feelings

Wednesday

no one knows

my rucksack

is empty

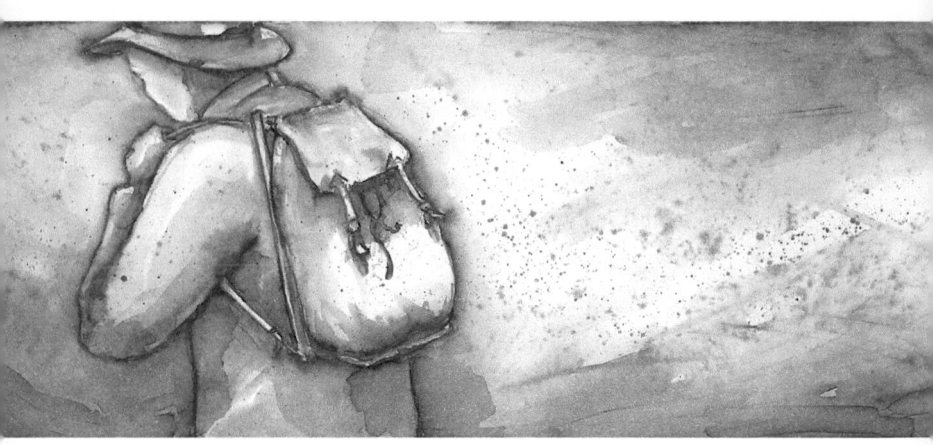

even in city streets

the smell

of linden

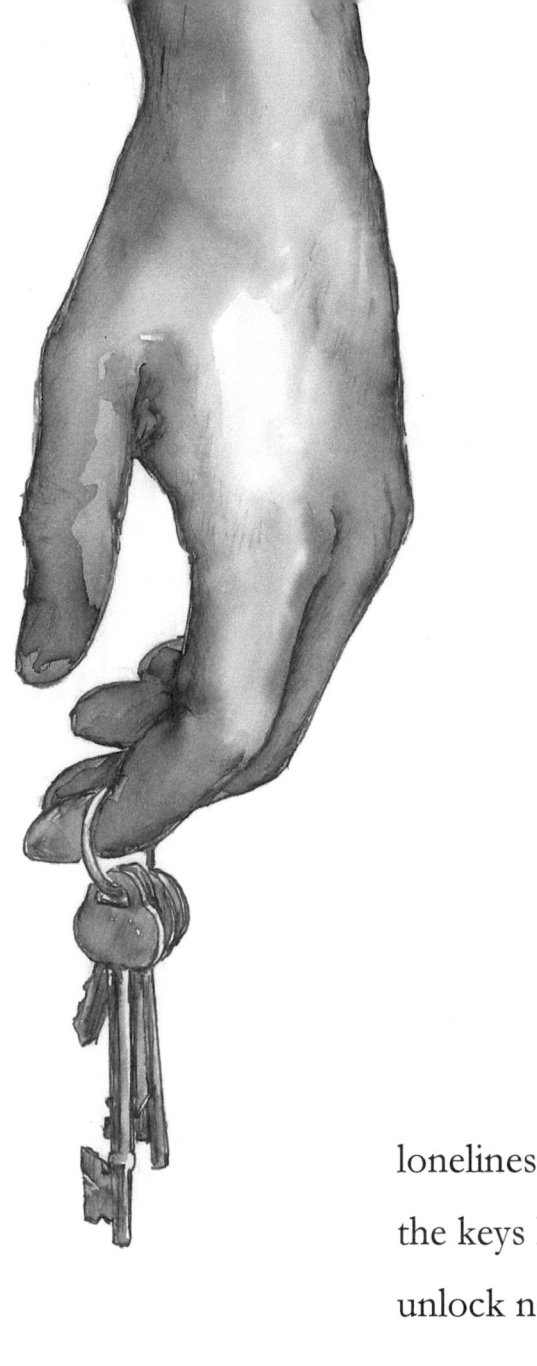

loneliness of streets

the keys I have

unlock nothing

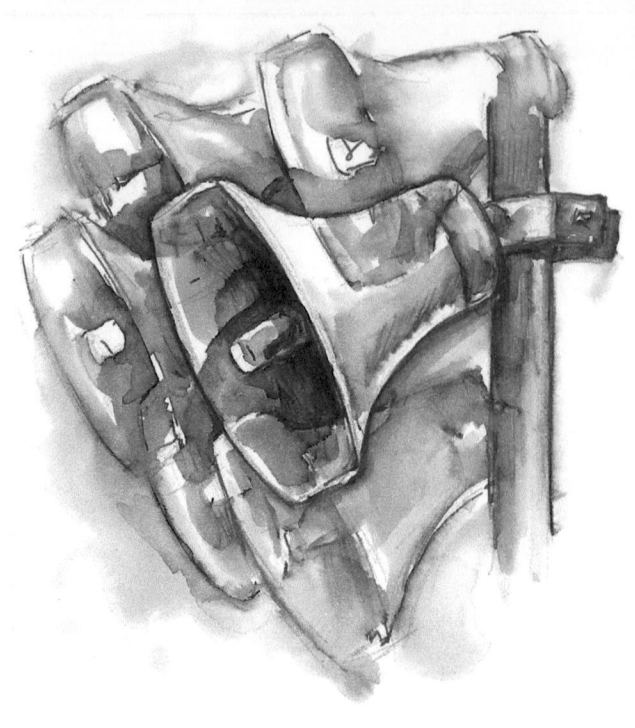

loudspeakers

in the train station

only echoes

smiling at me

two bikers

hand in hand

I stop to take notes

ducks flock

around me

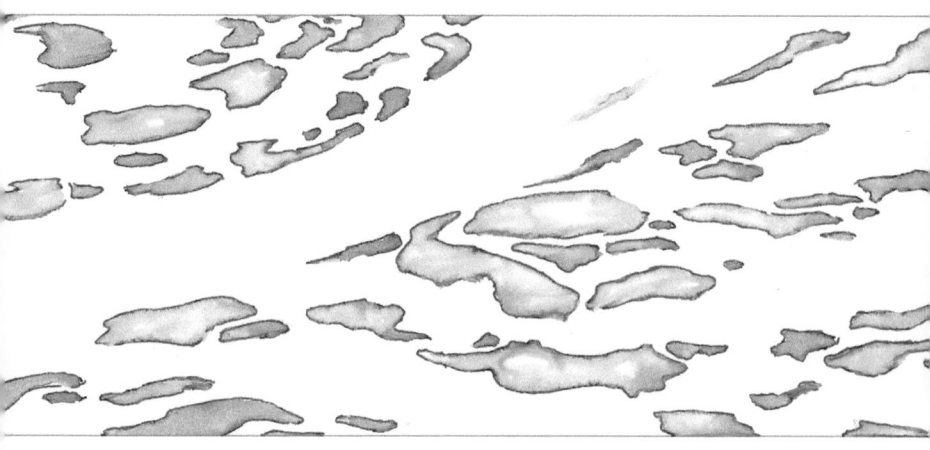

patterns of foam

a foreign alphabet

on the swollen river

lifeboat

lifeless

until needed

does the footbridge feel

sad and useless

when empty

a school of small fish

sealed in a drop

of boundless sea

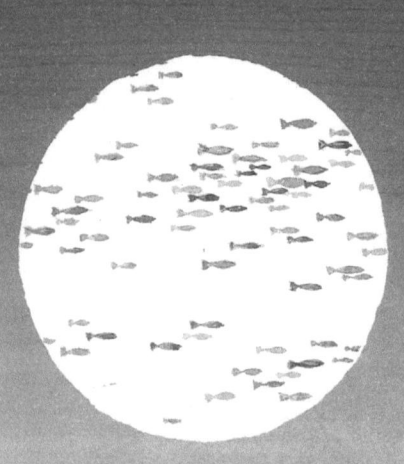

my quiet shadow

hears the tern catch a fish

or just miss

almost all panes gone

under the weight of nothing

the greenhouse bows

on the ant path

under an old oak

a wild egg broken and empty

airline sandwiches

opening around me

sound like rain

white people pay

to cross the ocean

packed like slaves

scarred

by skates

the spring ice moans

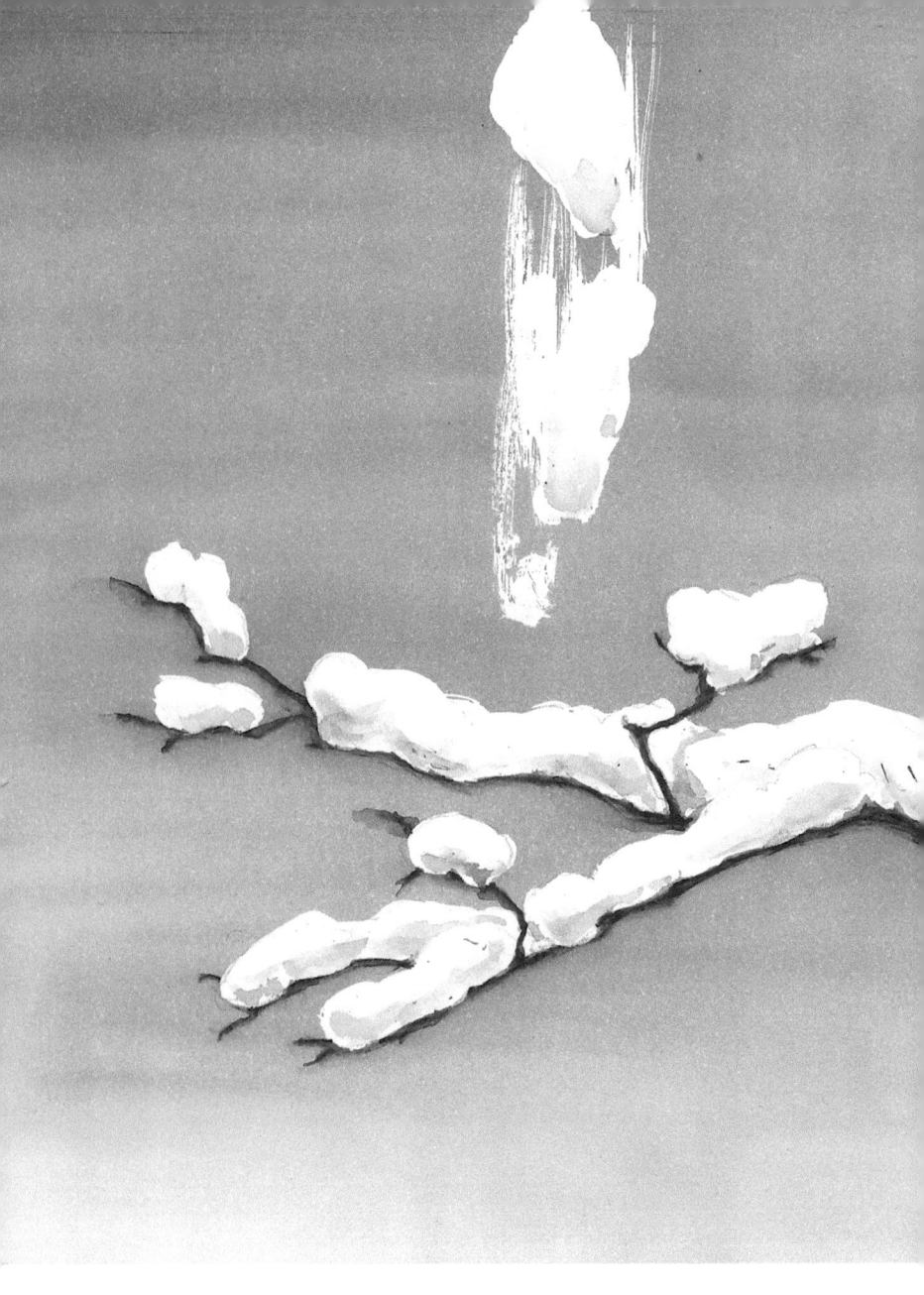

balancing

on bare boughs

a second snowfall

above snow drifts

on the minigolf course

a dangling pencil

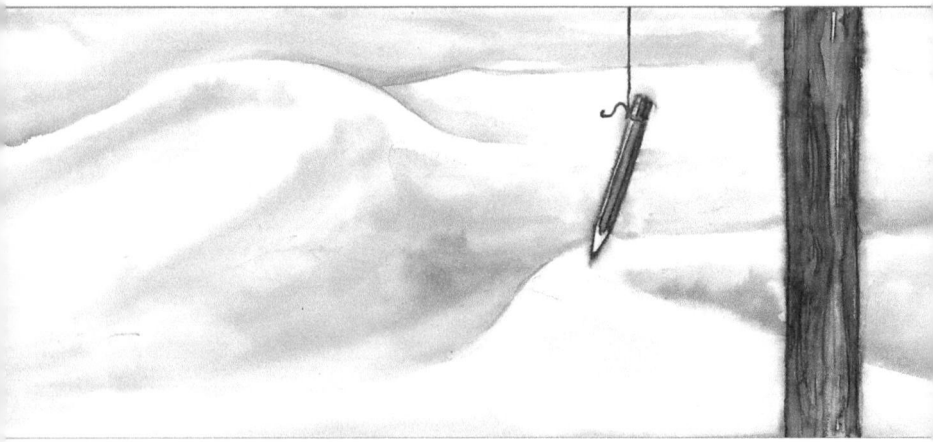

in the low sun

stubbled acres

glistening

brave winter bird

singing

to survive

last year's reeds

sleep

standing up

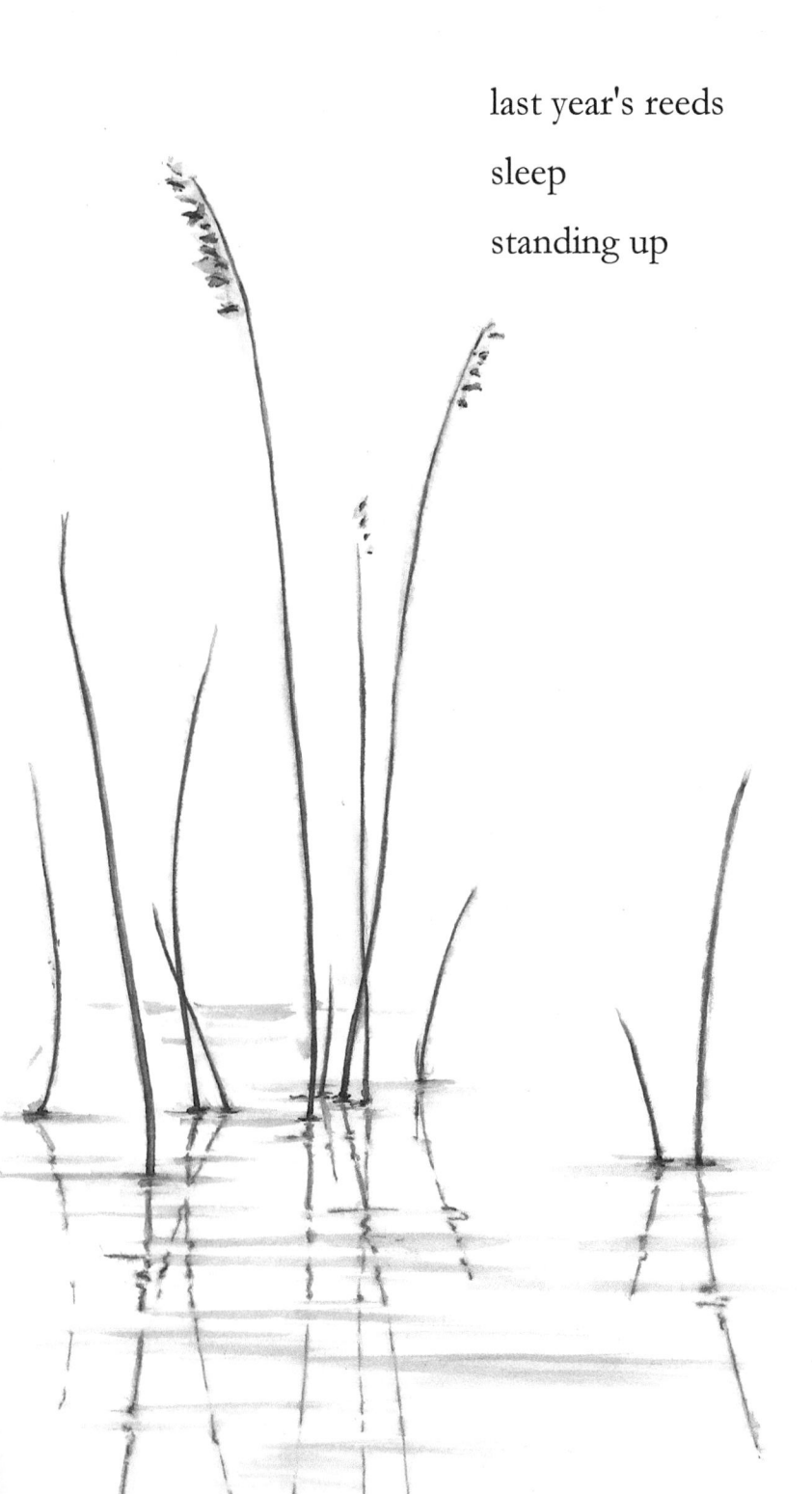

reading the paper

more interesting

over someone's shoulder

on their way to school

father and daughter

skipping

out forty floors high

optimistically weaving

skyscraper spider

scorched leaves

fall into the evening sky –

jackdaws

stumbling roots

congregate

on the forest path

brown on brown

moose cow

on a fallow field

electric fence

most often

bluff

in anticipation

of tasting my tea

my mouth forms a kiss

principally

I set my alarm clock

in order to sleep

a whirlwind

lifts the fallen leaf

back into its tree

in snow

I walk

the steps of others

love padlocked

on the cables of our footbridge

frosty and frozen

spring –

dandelion seeds

in a spider web

long ears
sneaking in the grass
a hare

winter sunup

lights of the office building

blink on one by one

in headwind

I talk

myself home

blanket of snow

over plowed fields

following the furrows

out on the furthest twig

a drop hesitates

in town a Sunday lull

along the shore

a rubble of stones

and the broken sounds of gulls

never heard a woman's voice

that couldn't, through practice,

become my home

every straw and stone

makes itself cozy

in the spring ice

in thaw

the waters moan and prod

to break out of their shell

temporarily darker

when the sun turns off

the street lamps

can't fix my day –

I'll let the day

fix me

spiders have gathered morning in their webs

every blade of grass has gathered dew

swallows have gathered on telephone lines

the road lies in shadows

ready for tires

a bumble bee kisses thoughtfully

old people in farm houses

lean toward their radios

trying to hear